SANTA LUCIA
BY STARLIGHT

SANTA LUCIA

BY STARLIGHT

POEMS

MICHAEL PEARCE

Brighthorse Books
13202 North River Drive
Omaha, NE 68112

ISBN: 978-1-944467-29-6

Cover Design © Mark McGowan
Cover Art © Charlotte Rossmann
Author Photo © Charles Carlson

Brighthorse Books is a small press based in Ponca Hills, Nebraska.
We publish poetry, short fiction, novels, and other books. For infor-
mation about Brighthorse Books, visit us at brighthorsebooks.com.

Brighthorse books are distributed to the trade through Ingram Book
Group and its distribution partners.
https://ipage.ingramcontent.com/ipage/li001.jsp

TABLE OF CONTENTS

MY FATHER'S BROTHER

The summers here are chilly, and the winters aren't anything,
and there's a dryness in the air but no smell. People are kind.
The workmen pound and cut in seven-hour shifts,
and eat their sandwiches at noon every day.

Even the hyenas wash the blood and shit from their teeth once a month
and saunter down to the post office to collect their checks.
Then they yelp among themselves in the town square,
or quietly taunt a passing schoolgirl.

Something happened in my family that shames me.
My father's brother shot a bank teller and got locked up.
In prison he found Jesus and learned songs that forgave
what he did. He's out now, and he goes to a church

where he sings those songs with other ex-cons.
There's a smell in that church—once you've been there
it rubs off on you forever. My girlfriend, who already knows
I'm my uncle's nephew, can smell me coming.

The fall is lovely here, like it is everywhere, full of golden light
and long meals and dimmed memories of the slights and wounds
        of summer.
The sorrowful eyes of old men knock each other around
like billiard balls until all they see turns red.

There's a story about my father and my uncle. They both loved the same girl
but my uncle loved her more. My father won her heart with a lie: he stole
        a love song
that my uncle wrote, and told her it was his, and she fell for it and married
        him.
My uncle left town, joined the army, murdered, went to prison, and came
        home loving Jesus.

It's not winter but the town is covered with a cloth as white as God's beard.
Burrowing owls and plovers splash in the dazzle of ashes that flutter down—
a haunting sight that everybody but me sees outside their window.
I look out and see the little boy across the street, walking crooked.

His dad got him a dog with huge jaws, and one Sunday morning
it chewed on his leg like it was licorice. Somebody killed the dog,
but it comes after the boy at night. When he wakes up gasping,
the only thing that calms him is biting down hard on a stick.

Sometimes I go to my uncle's church and watch him and the other guys
    sing and pray.
He goes on about how he was saved and absolved for shooting that bank
    teller
who had two daughters, but just look at him: he knows there's no forgiving
    father
up there making his agony of lost love and ruined lives melt away for a song.

The town square was designed by an architect who wanted us to walk and sit
with mindfulness, so he built hurdles on the walkways and glued bumps
    on the benches.
All the kids hang out in the old train yard, and leave the town square to the
    bums and hyenas.
Now there's a mall on the edge of town—they paved over the savanna to
    build it.

There's another story about my father and my uncle. When they were little
they would lie in bed together at night and decide what to dream, and the
    next morning
they'd compare notes. That's how they figured out they weren't the same
    person.
That's how they knew their hearts were tied together for eternity.

When I went to meet my uncle for the first time, my father stopped
    speaking to me.

2

GREAT BIG WOMAN

At eleven my mother was taller and stronger
than all the boys, and she pretty much stayed that way.
She had I-beam bones and a head large and hard
as a kettle gourd and a mouthful of big white teeth
with a gap you could drive a bus through.

The other kids hated her tallness and smartness
so she started smoking to stunt her growth
and flunked math on purpose. But she didn't
fool anybody so she gave up trying and became
an honor student and a basketball star.

She married a pale skinny man who is my dad.
She was so big and strong that when she laughed
my skin burned, when she yelled my eardrums rattled.
Sometimes my Noni and Grappa would
leave the house until she quieted down.

Once when she got mad she grabbed hold of me
and dragged me inside the house and shoved me
in a closet—her fingernails drew blood
and left little smiling scars on my arm.
That night she felt bad and sang me a lullaby.

When my dad left us, Mom went into her room
and cried for two days. She never spoke his name again.
For years I thought she'd killed him with the power
of her hatred, until one day he showed up at Smiley's.
By then he was so pale that most people couldn't see him.

At night, in bed alone, I could feel her bigness
all around me, like a sleeping bag that breathes.
She was the only person I was afraid of,
but she was always sweet to me at night,
so I always went to sleep feeling safe.

After she died last year she came into my bedroom—
I could hear her breathing and even smell her as
I slid into my dreams like a bullet loading into a gun.
I woke up to the sound of her singing: "Pony Boy,
Pony Boy, won't you be my Tony Boy . . ."

I will always be her Pony Boy riding across the plains,
and I'm still waiting for her to carry me
away to that little hill town beyond the ocean
where my Noni and Grappa lived until the Germans
marched in and burned it to the ground.

THE CRYING BOY

There's a boy in our town who cries all the time.
Since he's always crying
there's no telling what he cries about
he cries about everything.
That kid doesn't need a reason.

But the way that he cries—there's a subject.
On Sunday he shakes quietly,
his face screwed up like a wet question mark.
On Monday it's a squeal so high in pitch
you can be looking right at him
and not know he's doing it.
I won't bore you with the rest of the week
except to mention that on Friday
you'd best stay away from the crying boy.

It's hard to say why he shows up when he does.
We've no idea when to expect him.
He never uses Kleenex or a hanky.
He doesn't stay long.

He came by once
when we were eating dinner.
My sister and I chewed and watched him
squatting on the chair
his bare knees bulging like toad eyes.
I wondered when I'd first seen him,
was it in the school yard,
was it in church?
He swayed, slowly,
it made me sleepy to watch.
And it made me mad
to know that if I'd fallen asleep
I'd only have dreamed of the crying boy.

Once I saw the crying boy
in the aviary at our zoo.
He was staring at a South American Beaked Rainbow.
It was Sunday and he shook
like a horse covered with flies,
like an earthquake with brains.
He told me about a blind man led by a dog
only the dog is blind too he said
but it's okay because
it's the tension on the leash
comforts the man he said.
I said thanks for the story, Crying Boy.
Thanks for nothing.

That was last spring
but we still see him from time to time.
He's liable to show up anywhere in this town
and make a spectacle of himself,
sour the gutter with his tears.
I can't say I don't like the crying boy
when he talks, he sounds like an orgasm talking
when he talks, people pay attention
when he talks, words are lyrics to a stupid song everybody knows
a crying boy's words don't behave like normal words
they're like small fish huddled against the coral
rocking in a cluster to the ocean's drugged breathing.
I can't say I don't like the crying boy
and I can't say I'm not afraid of him.

Sometimes when the weather changes
I miss the crying boy
and try to picture where he is
and who is near him.

Sometimes I wonder what his bed is like—
is it cold and wet and smelly with mold?
If I peeled back the covers
and climbed into the crying boy's bed
would it be like slipping under the earth's slimy membrane
would my body soften like an old potato
would I fall asleep in the crying boy's bed
and sprout up other lives
that all have fun together
and don't remember me at all?
When I think about these things
I feel afraid of the crying boy.

But don't be fooled by the crying boy
he's no lighthouse in the storm
no rooster's crow.
He's only a child
who doesn't know right from wrong
and he sure doesn't know when to stop.
He cries about everything
he cries for nobody
and as far as anybody knows
he cries all the time.

NONI AND GRAPPA

My mother's parents came to our town
when she was six. They spent their money
on ship steerage and the train
that brought them west, and when
they got here they couldn't find work.

Mom used to say her parents started with nothing
but muscle and spleen and a language
so choked with throat-snot that its words
weren't spoken, they were coughed up.
Noni and Grappa were old when Mom was born.
As far as I know, they were always old,
but they got older and then older still.

They were short and wiry,
and Mom started out that way,
but after they got here Mom grew big
as a man from eating potatoes and corn-fed beef.
She went to Jefferson Grammar and Lincoln High
and fell for my dad, who wooed her with
a stolen love song, and they got married
on the archery range
at the foot of Pilgrim Hill
and had two kids, my big sister and me—
but that's another story.
This is about my Noni and Grappa.

Nobody would hire Grappa and Noni when
they came to town because they wore funny hats
and wool clothes and spoke an ugly tongue
that struggled up from their guts, a language whose words
mucked around in their belly, rattling against
kidneys and lungs and picking up

the stink and worry down there,
then climbed up a scaffold of ribs
into a throat that trapped those words
in a pit of tarry mucus.
Now and then the claw of anger
would reach down and grab a gob of them.

Nobody hired them so they borrowed
from McElroy and started a dry goods store.
At first nobody bought anything,
even though the prices were lower than Taylor's.
Then Grappa started making dolls with golden hair.
He carved the dolls from firewood and painted them
with colors made from dried flowers and dead insects,
and Noni sewed the clothes from pieces of dresses
that she had brought from the Old Country.
One by one she took out her old dresses
that she had carefully packed in her trunk,
cut them up and sewed them into much smaller dresses
and jackets and shirts and pants and even tiny socks and gloves.
She cut up her clothes from the Old Country
until all that was left was her wedding dress
and then she cut that up too.
Those tiny wedding dresses sold like hotcakes.

The hair of those dolls came from filaments
of stranded copper wire. Grappa
would poke six hundred and sixty-six tiny holes
in each doll head, and glue a single
copper filament in each hole
until there was a fountain of coppergold hair.
Every girl in town had to have one of those blond dolls.
Nobody on Mom's side of the family has ever been blond.

People bought the dolls with their little dresses,
and then they bought more clothes for the dolls,
and then they bought clothes for themselves,
and pots and skillets and garden tools
and light bulbs and electric heaters
and brooms and buckets and many, many
kinds of powder. The prices were lower than Taylor's
and eventually Taylor gave up and moved to Merced.

My Noni and Grappa didn't say much by the time I knew them.
As they got older the words from the Old Country
got harder to cough up. Those old words
stuck in the smoldering tar pit of their throat,
and without the words they couldn't remember the Old Country—
where it was or what it was called or what their little town looked like
or even who their own parents and brothers and sisters were.

One winter night years after my Grappa
had stopped making dolls and mostly sat
in the family room fiddling with the yellow pipe
he no longer smoked, I asked him what it was like,
the little town on the steppe that he had grown up in.
"Where was it," I asked, "what was its name,
was everybody small and dark and handy like you?
Give me something I can remember, Grappa," I said,
"because I will have children and grandchildren too."

I could see that he wanted to tell me something useful,
something that could unlock tears and light up darkness.
He coughed and coughed, trying to bring up the words he needed,
coughed until his face went purple and tears poured from his eyes.
And then *slurmp*, up came a fat clump of stuff
that sat on his tongue a moment,
then slid through his lips and plunked on his lap
like a newborn seal. It looked like a doll, but
without eyes or clothes or golden hair. I picked it up—
it was warm and green as jade and rubbery as molded Jello and

(I swear this on the grave of my not-so-dead mother)
it moved with the everslight ebb and flow of breathing.

I put it in my little jar that had held fish eggs
and I put the jar in the painted puzzle box
that I'd stolen from Billy Song.
My girlfriend once asked me
what was in the box, and I told her
it was a priceless jewel that my Grappa gave me.

All that coughing must have shaken Grappa's brain
in a bad way, because he didn't pay attention
to anything that had to do with words after that.
But he watched us, as we grew up and scrambled
for love and money, he watched us with interest
and a kindness in his eyes that my mother swore
had never been there before.

THE SEASONS OF SANTA LUCIA

Before Santa Lucia became our town
it was a Mexican town, or a Spanish town,
or an Indian town, or maybe all three.
And before that it was spackled together
by volcanoes and then a glacier cut through
the cool magma like a cake knife
and a bunch of earthquakes shuddered
and chewed and shrugged until the valley
lost all symmetry and purpose
except for the sweeping south crescent ridge
that God put up to protect us from
the itchy hunger of the savanna.
The crinkly terrain of our town
is cracked in half by a jigsaw creek that
gets lost in the coastal mountains
before it finds its way to the sea.

Many generations ago, before
my Noni and Grappa arrived here,
a man named Herman Dekker
took a boat down the coast,
way down and around the Cape Horn
and across the Atlantic and brought back
a zooful of African mammals and even
(so they say) some giant lizards.
They say he navigated the boat,
which we call Herman's Ark,
up the Santa Lucia River
and into our valley and on and up
through the Pyo pass to the savanna—
which is, of course, impossible.

Lorelei Schenk told me Dekker was a tulip farmer
who drove a team of four Friesian stallions
onto a ship in a village called Harlingen
in a country called Holland and sailed
to Nantucket and bought a big wood wagon
and headed west to dig for gold in
a California town called Rough and Ready.
He staked his claim and panned and rocked
and sluiced and dredged, then moved to our valley
and spent his dust and nuggets on a vast ranch
and started importing exotic carnivores.
Dekker would climb into his rig
and drive his horses to Frisco Bay
and come home with a wagonful
of bloodhungry beasts that he'd
turn loose on his ranch that sprawled
from Santa Lucia toward the savanna
but it had no eastern fence and those
orphan animals spread up and out
like rust on a tailgate.

Another story has it that Dekker
came along half a century later
and drove around the country hauling
a giant horse trailer from zoo to zoo,
twenty-nine of them in twenty-nine states,
and bought or stole animals from each one.
One way or another, our savanna has
some strange critters and sometimes they come
to our town and beg for sugar in
the parking lot across from the mall.

Our town sprang up on the south side
of the river but it sprawled over to the north.
For some reason white people with money
ended up on the north side, with the rest
of us stuck south. One autumn the rich northies
got together and paid three hundred Indians
to pray to God to bless their neighborhood.
And guess what: God's heavy hand
pushed down on the south side until it sank
below the level of the river, and the southies
had to build a long mound of mud and rubble
to protect their homes from the river;
but every now and then a flood
jumps the levy and reminds them of
God's greatness and gravity.

And guess what: when God's heavy hand
pressed down on the south side, the earth on
the north side swelled upwards,
making a wide majestic slope.
And the northies gave thanks
that their prayers had been answered
and their lovely homes could execute
their solemn guardianship of the town
perched like a parliament of barn owls
in their amphitheater over the river.

You should see the north side fences—
wrought iron and redwood,
pillared and picketed, simple and grand,
they are the pride of Hillside Heights.
We used to pile into Dad's pickup
every year on Christmas Eve
and drive up there and look at all
the colored lights and decorations.
Street after street was lit up like
a frozen party, with strings of lights
on the fences and little mangers

and wise men and Baby Jesuses
and farm animals and loudspeakers
blaring carols. McElroy's
nativity tableaus were
alive and moving—he hired
Mexicans to play all the parts.

When my mom was dying she pointed
north and whispered "I always wanted
a house there." She hoped I'd make a bundle
and go live on Hillside Heights. She said
"That's my final wish and blessing."

I never could afford a house
on Hillside Heights, and it's getting harder
to go visit there what with the recent
increase in gravity. But now and then
I'll still trudge up there after dark and peek
into a rich family's bathroom window
just to see if they shit the same
as we do. And sometimes late
on a soupy summer night I'll go sit
in a rich backyard and pet a rich dog
and fall asleep on the grass until
the watchman or the gardener or
the morning sun taps my shoulder
and says You better get going now—
and shame and gravity carry me home.

MAYOR BOB ON PILGRIM HILL

Mayor Bob is up on Pilgrim Hill in
the section where the war vets get buried.
He stands in a shower of gold light
waiting for guidance from the spirits.

His worries go beyond the council's
push and pull with law and money—
he's the shepherd of our town's soul
and he can smell the blood of the future.

Our mayor is short with a troubled look
and a walking stick for his own war wound
and sometimes a smile sets his face on fire
and we know he's found something we lost.

His wife Estelle has a smoker's cough
and her back is crooked from farm work.
She's often mad at Bob, but not
when he goes up to Pilgrim Hill.

The town is covered with purple clouds—
some would say it looks like rain.
But there's that shimmering chimney of light
on our mayor on Pilgrim Hill.

And there's a quiet as before a storm—
the bravest birds seek a lowdown tree.
Estelle is in the garden wondering
how she ended up with Bob.

When lightning strikes there's hell to pay
for Mayor Bob—he's knocked down flat
and shattered by a crackling beam
that burns a seam the length of his back.

Then the town feels something strange
like light or heat passing over us
and we know something has changed here
since Mayor Bob went up the hill.

When Bob walks back from the hill
of death his mouth's abuzz with new
ideas about how to save our town
from ruin, and who to sacrifice.

Now the birds have gone from our trees
and from our town. The bugs celebrate
everywhere you look, and children
fear their wrath and toe the line.

Mayor Bob doesn't leave
the house anymore. He speaks
to no one but Estelle, who issues
his decrees and cashes his checks.

They say that Bob saw something big,
that the sky opened over
Pilgrim Hill and Bob saw through
to something hot and vast and cruel,

that maybe that's what the Crying Boy
saw, and Danger Don too, as
his cursed T-Bird veered and flipped
off Slowdown Bridge and into the river.

I have never seen it, and won't
for a while, this sizzling something that
we shrink and make invisible with words
like death and God and eternity.

THE WALK OF COBBLED COINS

In our neighborhood the sidewalk got distorted over time.
The cold and heat cracked it and water roughed it up and tree roots
tilted whole squares of it until it looked like a long stripe of earthquake
running between the houses that plan and the cars that perpetrate.

Mayor Bob said we need a new sidewalk, so they plowed out the old one
and straightened the stripe. Mrs. Itzkowitz went from door to door
asking for change from everybody's change jars, and when they poured
          the concrete
the coins were set into it: the Walk of Cobbled Coins.

Those coins look like they fell out of the sky.
On a sunny day they shine like a river of stars.
You can almost hear their glimmer.
People come from all over town to walk on them.

Sometimes small children break their fingernails trying to pull
a quarter out of its socket. The older kids use sticks
and screwdrivers and Swiss army knives and
sometimes they manage to yank one up.

The Crying Boy once crawled the length of the block on his scabby knees
picking at the coins until his fingertips were bloody.
After that he just hung around dripping tears and snot
until the sidewalk got so slimy that my Noni slipped and broke her hip.

But once you've gotten a coin out of the Walk,
don't go thinking you're free and clear.
For some reason those coins never bring anything
good to anybody, and most people don't mess with them anymore.

My sister had a quarter from the Walk of Cobbled Coins
that she got from the boy across the street. They say
he pulled it up with his dad's skinning knife
the day before he disappeared into Anderson's house.

The boy across the street offered the quarter to my sister
to get the curse off his head. My sister wanted to help him,
so she took it to Anger's Garage where Henry Gutierrez fixed cars
and she glued it under the bumper of Danger Don's T-Bird.

In the fall the Walk of Cobbled Coins
whispers through the dead sycamore leaves.
If you put your ear to the ground you might hear
about nickels and dimes that were swiped and the lives they ruined.

Danger Don's funeral was a big noisy beer bash. My sister
demanded to say a prayer. She blessed Don
for taking the curse from the head of the boy
across the street, but nobody knew what she was talking about.

Some guy from Texas bought the T-Bird, cheap,
and drove off laughing about what a deal he'd got.
There are other loose coins floating around town—
I don't know where, or how much damage they've done.

THE THIRD PROPHECY

After lightning struck Mayor Bob
he sent out Three Warnings from his fever bed
that Estelle brought to the Town Council.
Since Bob couldn't talk it was understood
that these prophecies were Estelle's
version of what he was trying to say:

1. Beware of dark strangers hitchhiking through town.
2. Our children will rise up against us.
3. A great rain will come, and the drowning worms
will squiggle out of our ancestors' graves
and breathe a pestilence on Santa Lucia.

Everybody jumped on the first two,
even though 1 is a recipe for a lynching
and 2, well, isn't that pretty much
what old folks always foresee, and then
when it happens, which it always does,
they're shocked and say the world will end,
which it does, for them.
So the Council voted to prepare for 1 and 2,
but they decided that Estelle must have
heard Bob wrong on 3.

Even after the rains came and wouldn't stop
and the town became a shallow lake
and the water and gray sky sucked
the color from the countryside, even then,
with no end in sight, nobody recalled
the Third Prophecy. It wasn't until the deluge
reached Pilgrim Hill and all the bones
below the flood line decided they wanted
a second burial, a burial at sea,

but not before they danced and limped
and crawled through town leering
at the pretty girls and boys and
entering homes without knocking,
and the worms came up for air jabbering
obscenities that humans don't know
and can't hear anyway, squeaky little curses
that flew out over our town
with a message of spleen and contagion—
only then did we understand
that we were deep into 3.

The rich folks over on Hillside Heights
observed that the worst flooding happened
down on the South Side, and there was
an editorial in the Daily Dewdrop
titled South Side Sinners that blamed us
for all the misfortune that God rained down
on our town, and then Father Pat chimed in
in one of his sermons and even
Rabbi Cohen wondered if
the Siders were the cause of this
great gushing pestilence—
as though nobody had ever told them
that water runs downhill.

The Council sent the health department
to inspect the flooded structures
and they condemned four of them for
being chock full of plague and then
Sheriff Roy brought in some forestry guys who
torched them then stood by in the rain with hoses
to make sure those buildings died alone.
One of them was across from our place,
was the old barrel warehouse where
Henry Gutierrez welded his steel horses.
Henry sat at our kitchen window
and drank wine with my dad and watched

that building burn to the ground until
all that was left was a rabble of horses
whose tortured metal skin was smoke black
splotched with iridescent rainbow hues.

After that the Town Council decided
enough was enough and they let nature run
its course as the great flood that had nearly
drowned all hope and reason petered out and
Henry Gutierrez got sick but he recovered

and that's my childhood: a mishmash
of sorrow and light, fluttering in
the wake of God's sloppy experiment.

SEASON OF WORMS

It was the year of endless rain, when we finally learned
how to smell as our eyes shrank and our ears surrendered
to the foamy white noise of water.
It was the year the brown hillsides found the courage
to give birth to their own fragile hope,
while the river came back with a vengeance,
reversed its course and dragged in sea creatures
and stories of wily sirens and drowned mariners.
It was the year our town's dead ancestors moved back in
with their families, hounded our parents with their
dumb toothy naggings, picking bits of flesh and sinew
from their own ribs and chewing on them like dogs.

The parents of Santa Lucia spent so much time indoors
that they lapsed into a rut of useless tradition.
They made us kids learn manners they'd long forgotten,
the same manners that the columns of marooned ants
practiced in the dry refuge of our town's kitchens.
They were always praying now, these fussy parents—
they prayed back the old gods, the ones who'd
stirred up rivers and lakes with their pompous dance,
who'd wagged their league-long hair
and hurled boulders at mountains.
But those ancient gods came back to this world
with only half their old powers, they were
tired now and confused, like people.

Each time our parents bowed their heads
my sister and I tiptoed away. We'd find Lenny or Ida
or Billy and go splashing barefoot through swollen gutters,
laughing and flapping our drenched shorts
in a dance that spilled out of last night's dream.
Our naked shoulders purpled in the downpour

but we tromped on through soggy brown leaves,
through spaghetti orgies of worms who'd shed
all modesty as they floated up from underground.
All around us parents watched from foggy windows
and cursed the prodigal sky while dead ancestors
stood behind them clapping their grubby hand bones
and clanging rib cages together in obscene percussion.

The grownups knew that they had brought this rain,
that their hearts had clogged up like old pipes,
a rage of tears piling high and higher
until they spilled out of the sky and
onto the parched streets of our town.
We kids figured out that the mud
must have come from their bowels,
the heavy air from their lungs,
the tulips and daffodils from flashes of lust
that streaked downward from their hearts.

The youngest kids had grown up with only drought,
for them this baptism was a blurred memory
of a womby paradise long since baked away.
For them each new day was a door opening
into a hazy room filled with the din and stink
of displaced animals, each night a black canvas
shimmering with black stars and a fierce black moon.

The flood swelled and gushed and washed all plans
clean away as the hours chewed up ambitions
and spat them into the streets, mocking parents
in front of their howling kids.
The mold that grew in plaid patterns on bathroom walls
glowed green then yellow then fluorescent orange,
then belched its toxic spores into the air.
So much of the landscape had been brushed gray
that we couldn't tell a treetop from a cloud—
sometimes we thought our eyes must have healed over.
The days loitered, the months refused to budge.

It was in mid-July that we, the triumphant children,
suddenly got so melancholy you could hardly tell
we were breathing. We stopped going outside,
put on hats and shoes and disapproving faces
and sorted our toys into categories—
and that was when the grownups understood
that the rain had given over to a dead blue sky.
They walked out into the world of bright and shadow
and celebrated with beer, left us in a cage
littered with rotting ancestors. And there we grieved
and languished as they gave thanks to the new season
of distinctions and clean grace.

ROILING HEARTH

It's not the town it was is what
I hear some cranky old folks say.
They talk about the mall that once
was a bog full of coots and egrets and ducks
and swallows and red-winged blackbirds and
they talk about the apple orchards
and plum and walnut groves and
vineyards to the west of town
that use to be a great wavy slope
awash with oak and tamarack pine
coyote bush and gophers hares and deer.
And they say the summers were warmer
the winters colder the mountains higher
and the men and women less afraid.

Used to be the mayor was a war hero
the sheriff was a baseball star
even the dogcatcher had climbed
the highest mountain in Argentina
and planted the flag of our town up there.
You look at the old photos and see
people who are different from us,
whose coats were cut from timeless cloth
whose arms and legs seem more at home
whose eyes look more certain and fierce.

And the river—the roiling hearth
of our town that quenched our fields
and brought in bass and trout and carried
away our garbage, and if you trust
the murky codgers and hazy hags
who chatter in the town square
the river was a long swift train

through a treacherous corridor
to an endless sea of mythobeasts
and mariners, of birds that zag
from pole to pole and islands that spout
their highfalutin principles
all the while playing footsie
with each other down below ...
Where was I? Oh, the river, yes,
that old snake river that
was once a conduit and touchstone
now mostly sits there and stinks,
a filthy moat between rich and poor.

My Aunt Rachel told me sure,
it was different then, but she
will never miss the washboards and clotheslines
the woodstoves and polio and whooping cough
the funerals with tiny coffins and
the schoolmaster's stern yet creepy hand.
And my old Noni remembers worse
from the Old Country that she won't even
talk about, and I don't blame her.

TRACK STAR

Dorsell Quivers ran like a bow
chasing its own arrow.
Aunt Rachel used to say he ran like the dogs
were after him, but anyone could see
he didn't care what was behind him.
He was running after something
invisible to Aunt Rachel and me
but he saw it and knew it was important.

When he wasn't running he'd still wear
his track jersey to show off his shoulders,
and he wore red sweatpants and army boots
with the laces untied and always
he had a silver chain around his neck
with a locket made of silver and ivory
that Lorelei Schenk said contained
a picture of his mother, a white woman
who died when he was a baby.

His dad Walter and his half-sister Ida raised him,
and every day after school he had to help his dad
fix vacuum cleaners before he did his homework.
Ida cooked dinner and Walter said grace—
it was a prayer the old man had made up in which
he thanked the Lord for a long list of things
that included sparing him from "the lash
of the chicotte" and "the iron manacles of slavery."
Dorsell always smiled to himself
because all he was thankful for were
his two powerful legs and his sister's chicken stew.

He first started running when he was seven.
When he was twelve something went haywire

and he couldn't make his legs move faster than
a languid, burdened shuffle. His dad took him
to a doctor, who said it was mental, so
he took him to the Witch Lady who told him
Drink this tea and tell your legs
to cast off their irons and walk free.

He did as he was told, and in a few weeks
he was running like a gazelle.
He got better and better at running
and then he started winning prizes.
That didn't sit well with Walter—
Lorelei said something in his heart snapped
and he went sour. He told Dorsell
he didn't want him wasting his energy
on running like a trained greyhound,
he wanted him doing useful work
that put food on the table.
Then Walter went down to Lincoln High
and made them take Dorsell off the team.

Up till then Dorsell had been a pretty good son
but now he changed too. He went up against his dad,
said it was his destiny to run and nobody could stop him.
They yelled at each other, and Walter struck Dorsell
with his fist. So Dorsell picked up a pipe wrench and
slammed Walter on the head. Walter could never
walk right or think straight after that.

Dorsell quit school, and he and Ida
took over the vacuum repair business,
and they both take care of Walter now.
In the early mornings Dorsell runs in the foothills
along the edge of the savanna valley.
He can run for hours, and sometimes
he'll chase a deer or rabbit
until it drops from exhaustion,
then spit in its eye and laugh.

Every now and then at the beginning
of deer season some hunter
will spot Dorsell up there,
running with the deer and elk.
McElroy's cousin Jody says he almost
shot Dorsell last August—somehow he
mistook him for a Columbian black-tail
and had him in his scope and started squeezing
out a shot when he recognized him.

Dorsell and Ida take Walter to church
most Sunday mornings. Ida sings in the choir,
and Walter sits up front with Dorsell
and says, a little too loud,
"That's my girl, my good child,
sings like a bird in a dragon tree.
The boy, well he fell to the wayside,
we lost him to a life of drink and ruin,
for all we know he's perished and got himself
a gig sharpening the Devil's teeth."

And Dorsell puts on his prideful smile
and listens to Ida and the other singers
swaying together in their violet robes,
and their shimmering four-part harmony
washes over him—and maybe Walter too—
like a shadow, or a flood, or the stampede of
a thousand hooves over the savanna.

ANDERSON'S CHICKEN

The boy across the street walks in his sleep.
He'll putter around in his bedroom, or he'll go
down to the basement and get into the gun cabinet.
He likes to clean the Remington 11-87 or
cock and pull the trigger on the unloaded Browning Rimfire.

Or he'll start talking, using real words,
but you wouldn't recognize them on account of
they've been disguised with new meanings
so you can't understand a single sentence.
When he wakes up he never remembers what he did or said.

One Monday he walked right out of his house
and on down the Walk of Cobbled Coins with that limpy gait of his.
He walked on pennies and nickels and dimes
past the neighbors' pebble driveways
and brick driveways and green concrete driveways
until he came to Anderson's place, which he entered
through an unlocked side door.

He was there for a week, but nobody knew it.
Everybody was looking for him until
the chief of police said he must be dead.
Then late the next Monday night Jeff Thompson
saw him leave Anderson's by the same side door
and head for home. When he saw Jeff he said
"The core, it ran stab on into it, the core, the core, and under"
and he walked up his own front walkway and onto the porch,
and lay down and sang himself a lullaby, and went on sleeping.

They arrested Anderson and took him to the station
and they beat him up some, but he said he didn't know anything.
Then they started holding his head under water
until he told them what they wanted to hear.

The next week the boy across the street got red spots
on his behind and his tummy and dreamed he was chased by cheetahs
and panthers and other animals he'd never seen before,
not even on TV, and he woke up screaming.
He kept walking in his sleep.
He walked down to Anderson's again,
and over to the side door and tried to get in,
but it was boarded up now. So he just lay down there,
sang a lullaby, and slept like a hibernating bear.

Five years after he was hauled away
Anderson got released from prison.
The boy across the street, who was a teenager now,
sent him a letter with pictures of himself
and his best friend Phate playing in their band.
"Phate plays drums," he said, "and I write all the songs."
Anderson never wrote back. He lives with his mother
in the northwest corner of the Four Corners region
where he has a job sexing chickens
on a nearby farm and plays gin rummy
with his mom and her church friends on Thursday nights.

The boy still walks in his sleep, and talks, and fiddles with guns.
The songs he writes for his band come from his dreams.
When he's writing a song, he begins with the chords,
and then he puts together the notes of the melody.
Then all of a sudden he'll remember a dream,
and he'll start singing in that crazy sleep language of his,
lyrics full of familiar words that don't belong together—
they have been called together for a new purpose,
they have been made dangerous, the way the words
of a judge or a king are dangerous. When you hear them
you feel itchy, or fondled, or double-crossed,
or abandoned in some empty forlorn place,
and then you want to hear the song again,
and then again, just one more time.

CRICKET MAN

Billy Song's father had a name
I couldn't pronounce, and I couldn't
understand him when he talked,
and I didn't like the whine of his voice
or the shrill music of his language and
I didn't like the smells in the Song house either.

Sometimes Billy and I snuck out
of marching band together and slunk
around town, eating candy and reading comics
at Greeko's store because Greeko wouldn't
rat you out as a truant as long as you spent money.

Sometimes we climbed up to the attic
of my house and went through the stack
of my father's dirty magazines,
staring at the same breasts my father stared at
and touching our spazzy penises.

Once when we were in his backyard
I tried to open the door to the little shed there
but Billy told me his dad didn't let him in there.
We peeked in the window but couldn't see much
in the dark. "He makes cages," Billy said.

Then one Saturday I went over there
and his father said Billy was off
at his trombone lesson. I didn't want to
stick around but his dad took my arm
and led me back to the shed and unlocked the door.
It was a strange sight: all these tiny cages,
dozens of them woven from bamboo strips,
were hanging from the ceiling.

33

Each one held a single cricket, and all
those crickets chattered like a schoolyard.

Billy's dad showed me a gourd with Chinese letters on it
and a lid he'd carved from rosewood and ivory.
"Carry crick," he said, and then again, "carry crick,"
his words coming from some whiny place
in his throat and nose, higher up and lighter
than the bellyburble of my Noni and Grappa.

He opened one of the bamboo cages
that hung over the workbench, and
took out the biggest insect I ever saw.
"Big China crick," he said, "fight tough."
He put it in the gourd and pushed in the lid.
"Carry crick to fight tonight,
tear Japan crick to pieces."

I nodded and backed away towards the door,
but he grabbed my arm quick. "I teach you," he said.
I shook my head and tried to leave
but he held on tight. "Billy no my son," he said.
"Son of udda man. I know, say nothing,
so no have kill udda man. Billy no my son.
I no give crick secrets to Billy. I give you."

He wouldn't let go. He said
"You pick one crick, take home."
I found the smallest cage with a little
bug inside and said I'd take it.
"No take that one," he said.
"Good sing but no fight."

"You said pick one," I said. "It's mine."
He looked me hard in the eye, but
let go of my arm. "Beautiful sing."
He told me to feed it by chewing beans
and sheep liver and spitting them on a dish.

"You no tell Billy what I tell you.
He know nothing. You go home."

I never went to Billy's house after that, and
when I quit the marching band our friendship ended.
I kept my cricket, fed her bean cud,
and she sang me to sleep until the night she died.
Lorelei Schenk said Billy's father left the family
and went back to China. His mother never remarried
but she went on loving Futoshi Sato,
the mechanic at Anger's garage.

BEST FRIENDS

When Lenny Schacter disappeared
twelve years ago nobody knew
where he went, though there were rumors.
His sister thought he was dead,
but his mother had faith that
some sweet day he'd come home rich.

Sure enough he rolled into town
in a new Escalade and headed straight
to Cliff Hanger Real Estate and paid
cash for a house on Hillside Heights.
Belinda Rey who manicures McElroy
said Lenny opened a bank account
with forty million and change.

We were buddies from the day
Lenny and his mom and sister moved
to town and rented the house next door.
He and I played tetherball
and mouthed off to Miss Bruner
in arithmetic and later on
at Lincoln High we both kissed
Belinda Rey at the bowling alley.

Lenny made his millions in
TechTown, three valleys over,
building computers for cars and phones
and televisions. When he came home
he bought up land on the South Side
of the river, including the dump
I live and work in. And he fixed
the levee so his properties
wouldn't flood in any storm.

He hired me to remodel his kitchen
and then to make a table and chairs
and then a chest of drawers and a bed.
But things were different now, he was
my boss and nothing more. Only
there *was* more, he had a score
to settle, or maybe he'd become
a different person. He'd meet with me
once a week to inspect my work,
then he'd shrug and write a check,
sighing like I hadn't earned
the money he was paying me.

The thing is, I did Lenny bad
way back when. We were walking
home from Jefferson Grammar
and there were the Kronman boys
at Piglet Park with Lenny's sister
Grace, trying to make her eat
a snail. Lenny was ready to fight
but I stopped him. We stand with the boys,
I said, Grace is the enemy.
I made him pour dirt on her head and call her
a filthy dog, which he did.
He shook with a fury then, and I
knew he wanted to rip out my tongue
but he just kicked his sister and ran.

Next time I saw him he had two
Big Hunks and he gave me one.
He said he'd taken it from Grace
on the way to school that morning
and then he laughed loud and short
but there was murder in his eyes.

Somehow our friendship grew stronger—
I would even call it love,
and it stayed that way until

the Great Storm broke the levee
and flooded the South Side, wrecking
our homes—that's when Lenny skipped town.
I used to see his sister Grace
at Lincoln High sitting alone
in the lunchroom—then I hated
Lenny, and I hated myself.

THE DOG AT THE EDGE OF TOWN

There's a dog down the road
waiting for me. She wants to play,
to take me to the pine forest of her youth
and feed me chewed-up rabbit meat
and fetch anything I throw.
But if I try to walk on past her
her growl is full of murder,
as if all the world beyond
is her den of precious pups.

There's a dog down the road
named Randy, or maybe it's Rags.
I visit him in my flip-flops and shorts
and he licks my scabby knees,
then rolls over on his back,
legs stretched fore and aft. I rub
his belly and the pink slug of his penis
pokes out of its hairy sheath.

There's a dog across town
at the Home for Old Jewish Ladies
who sits on the porch and watches when
I bring Aunt Rachel her mail and chocolates.
He bows and wags as I head up
the walkway, then bam, the little fuck
goes apeshit, bares his fangs
and cranks up the bass in his growl.
He bit me once, so now I carry
a spray can and if he charges
I blast his Judas mug.

There's a dog in that tree. She's tired
of running, wants to fly like a bat,
plucking bits of flesh from the air.
She sits up in a crotch of limbs
and hums a human song, waiting
for the nerve to flout gravity
and step out on a terrace of dreams.

There's a dog at the edge of town
who doesn't speak dog, his yammerings
a mix of goat and donkey and some owl.
The other dogs keep away—they don't get
what he's saying and they want no part
of him. Once a posse of three
ambushed him behind a barn and
chewed him up pretty good.
What's he gonna do, move out
to the savanna and chum up to hyenas?
He still keeps an eye on the others,
hoping to make friends.

There's a hydrant on the corner
that's been splashed with a century's worth
of desires and hopes. It stands proud
as a tombstone, its memories written
in stinky rust, in the air around it,
in the yelps of newborn pups.

There's a wolf in that stand of pines.
She opens her mouth to yap and howl,
but all that comes out is a meek boy's voice.
He says "Help," that little boy, says it quiet,
like he's talking to himself,
swaddled in the belly of that wise beast.
Sometimes it's a steady, smoldering
anger—"Help, help, help, help,"
because he knows nobody's listening.
Sometimes he coos the word

with a baby's idle cheer,
"Helpy-yelp, helpy-yelp,"
that's all giggles and sighs.
Then one day he's inspired
and he shoves his fist up the throat
of that smug beast and she explodes
with a brand-new noise—
"Wolf!" she cries, "wolf, wolf!"
and for the first time ever a dog is born.

There's a dog in our dreams, yours and mine,
that scampers back and forth between us
carrying secret messages
that we forget when we wake up.
Day after day we look at each other
and can't remember what we want to say
as our noses worry the air
and our love howls louder, year upon year.

THE MUSIC KIDS SAIL TO A DISTANT SHORE

My Noni and Grappa didn't talk much
about where they came from or how they got out
but one time we were sitting on a blanket
at Limbo Lake eating tangerines and watching
a bunch of kids from Jefferson Grammar
pile into a canoe that kept tipping over
and it reminded Noni of a group of Jewish kids
at the Varna Port all filing onto a rickety boat
to sail south on the Black Sea before the bloody claw
of the Reich could grab them and feed them to the
beast of Germany. She watched them standing
on the deck in their dark wool coats waving
to their doomed parents. "So strange it was
to see the children float away into
that chilly fog, that unknown future."

When the music kids first formed a group
they asked me to join them because
I was the best musician in ninth grade
except for Herschel Gould who played violin
in the grownup orchestra and had once
gone to the capital and won third place
in an all-state youth competition.

I told the music kids I was too good
to play with the likes of them but maybe
someday when they get better I'll
give them a shot. They were a bunch of
dreamy dorks anyway. I continued as
first clarinet in the marching band and
the music kids kept their combo alive
with little lunch concerts and parties
and such until they got pretty good,
so I told them they were ready for me now.

They said no thanks, they didn't really
need a clarinet though a saxophone might
do the trick, so I stole my Grappa's camera
that he never used and traded it at the BSL
pawn shop for a crummy Brazilian alto sax
and spent four months learning to play it
and then I went to the music kids and
told them I was ready to join them
but by then Jeff Kronman had gotten his
driver's license and they'd found a pretty
good sax player over in Pewter City
and rehearsed at his place once a week
and there I was, a music kid reject.
Not long after I quit the marching band.

That's when I remembered Noni's story
about those refugee kids getting on the boat
that would take them to their future and
I understood then that there are boats
in the harbor of childhood and they linger
for a while until some kids jump on
and pretty soon they cast off because
boats need to set sail and so do kids,
and I started to notice that these boats
were one by one taking off without me
and I felt I'd been left behind and
there I was standing by the harbor and
I wasn't quick enough to hop onto
a newly arrived boat so I just stood there
watching boat after boat shrink into the fog.

I never caught up with the music kids
I just shuffled around the piers and pilings
of that stupid metaphor of a harbor
until one day I was sweeping sawdust
at Fred Lambert's mill when I noticed
old Rick Cummings debarking the grizzled bole
of a fat walnut tree from the Joost Grove

this side of the savanna. Rick fed the log
through the headsaw that split it down the middle,
opened it up like a book and there it was,
the purplish-brown face of my destiny,
flat as a flag yet deep as a forest,
tough enough to last but amenable
to jointer knives and sawblades and
the imagination of a lonely kid
whom music had left for dead.

One day not long after my mom died
I was digging around in her basement
and there was my black watersnake
of a clarinet in pieces in its mildewy case
with its dull metal keys and rods.
I put the pieces together and suddenly
I knew it different: somebody had
crafted it from ebony and nickel
and it felt warm in my hands like
I was touching the hands that made it
and I felt a special closeness
to my old clarinet and the tree
and earth and air and light
and care that had composed it.

DOC

He bought a big house at the end
of Oak Street, but he's never there.
Weekdays he's at his office, healing
coughs and wounds, but other times

he's in Smiley's at his table
by the wall, where he sits
with a bottle and a glass
watching the Gladiator Channel.

He drinks like there's no tomorrow
which, of course, is technically true.
He drinks like there's a prize at
the bottom of the bottle, a model

ship or a gold ring, or a note
from himself when he was a boy,
or a tiny bottle of much stronger
stuff. He never acts drunk.

His father made him learn science,
made him come home every day
right after school and study hard.
He saved up dimes and quarters in

a jar to buy a bicycle,
but when Mrs. Itzkowitz came collecting
change for the Walk of Cobbled Coins
his father gave the jar to her.

The way he sets a broken bone
is he imagines how it broke
then runs it backwards, his mending hands
shearing in reverse, a savage

rumble churning underneath
his quiet voice. When Noni
cried about her cancer pain
he told her to keep it to herself.

When the Thompson boy, the retard,
shot up like a weed and started bothering
the girls at Lincoln High, the town council
paid Doc to cut off his huevos and got

the kid a job at Gleason's warehouse.
He doesn't bother anybody
anymore. Sometimes he visits
Doc and looks at his balls in a jar.

They say when Doc was young he fell
for a girl who loved him for a month
or two, but she was too wild for Doc.
He cried for weeks when she dumped him,

and hasn't cried since. His father
is buried on Pilgrim Hill. He never
knew his mother. He sleeps downstairs
in his big house, on the couch.

McELROY THE BANKER

He chews his stogie's sour cud
and stands apart from all of us
a man amused by petty squabbles.
Way back when he gave Aunt Rachel
a mortgage with no money down
saying he likes to lend to Jews,
it's a good bet, but I think
he just liked Aunt Rachel, his
chosen person. . . . And maybe liked
to see the ancient tribe step up and on
and over the Christian bully boys
who flicked his ears in church who
taunted him on the baseball diamond
who never let him up from under
the fat corpse of his bad beginning
and so he chose to plod alone
to the bitter end of the rainbow
which is wealth and death and if
that's not enough a knowledge
that history's atrocious blight
cannot be touched or forgotten and
if that's not enough an eternity
without the poison eye of Jesus.

McElroy's a fine old boy
a lonely goy an old maid's toy
he's loaded to the gills with gelt
a gefilte fish out of water.

He'd never admit his cross to bear is
ordinary, no better and no worse than that
he once had zilch in a church of much but
scraped and pinched and clawed until

47

his dinner came up roses and the girl
of his dreams who'd married a mortician
cut his hair and buffed his nails and
his nemesis the quarterback owed him
thirty years of toil and this year
he's the guest of honor at the Farmers'
Fall Harvest Bash and even Rabbi Cohen
pays him well in fawning gapes and grins ...
And yet his life goes limp each spring
when breezes bite and roses bud and
dewdrops dingle on the pane and
all that's green and fresh and poised
pulls him to a troubled time
to an undone man in the hide of a boy
who craved a dad he never got
to guide him through a village that
didn't need him, that showed him the door
to a mean and cold outside and to
the sepulcher of his success.

McElroy's a fine old boy
a lonely goy an old maid's toy
he's loaded to the gills with gelt
a gefilte fish out of water.

OLD DAVE IN SAVANNALAND

There's an old guy who lived on the edge
of Savannaland. I used to see him
sometimes, when I was out there with
some homegrown ganja and my dad's rifle.
I brought the rifle along for the hyenas,
though people say they're too tame
to attack—they have it too good
to queer the deal of their lazy indenture.
I brought the ganja to help me imagine
Savannaland as it was before there were
guns or words or people.

When I first saw him, from a distance,
I thought he was younger. He
was hiking in his army shorts
with his rucksack and canteen
and a downunder hat and
a carving knife strapped to his leg.
He noticed me but marched on
without a word or wink as
we passed on the trail, inches apart,
and I could see from his skin that he
was as old as my Grappa.

I never saw him up close again,
at least not in Savannaland.
Sometimes I'd spot him high on the bluff
staring out at the raptors that hover
near the hillside to catch the rising
currents of air. He always looked
like he was talking to those hawks
and falcons, telling them about
the loves of his youth or the deaths
of his wife and daughters and son.

Once I saw him skinning a rabbit
with the carving knife—
it looked like a naked pink baby
with furry boots and a fur hat.
He spied me across the creek
and his eyes held me with a gaze so cold
I felt like just another animal on the hill.

It took me years to figure out
the savanna guy was Beggar Dave.
That's because of his disguise—
in town he wore a bushy gray beard,
a soiled robe and bedroom slippers,
and stood bent over
like an engine hoist
muttering his drunken jabber.
Song's Grocery used to give him
cookies and chips and peanut butter.
The rest of us gave Beggar Dave money—
it was bad luck not to—and Dave
always took your coin and
moved it in the figure of a cross
and blessed you and your family.

I saw him in the town square,
where nobody goes anymore,
saw his skin and eyes up close.
I asked him if he had a twin
in the hills around the savanna
but he shouted at me to go away.

Then last fall Dorsell Quivers
was chasing a deer near the rim
above Savannaland when he came upon
a cave in a shady dell.
All around the mouth of that cave
were stakes pounded in the ground,
scores of them, each with the rotting head

of a hyena. Old Dave was sitting there
spooning peanut butter out of a jar.
He saw Dorsell and grabbed his knife
and took after him, but
nobody can catch Dorsell.

The next morning, when Dorsell led
Sheriff Roy to the cave, Old Dave
was gone. No one's seen him since.

THE LIGHT CHANGED

Lenny and I were heading southeast
toward the savanna with our slingshots
looking for squirrels and lizards when
the air suddenly hushed dead still
as the light shrank to an icy blue.
We looked at each other and giggled but
when we looked back out to Razor Ridge
we were blinded by a blaze
of colors that tore through our eyes
and lit up the backs of our skulls
like a rainbow from another galaxy.

We closed our eyes and waited, and when
we opened them again the light was
not so bright but still packed with colors
we had never met before and as we stared
toward the southeast rim that we now call
Rainbow Ridge there appeared a troop of hyenas
escorting a huge rhinoceresque creature—
the light blasted through its skin like
a cheap window shade and there were
its bones trotting along inside it looking
like the skeleton of a giant dog with
a double-dagger nose and a big-ass grin
full of Halloween teeth and satisfaction.

We couldn't tell if the hyenas were escorting
that rhinomonster to some limestone throne
up there on Dekker's Peak or to its
execution by plummet from the summit
and we decided not to stick around and see
since the monster or its escorts
might take an interest in us, a couple
of twelve-year-olds with slingshots.

We found out later that everybody in town
was caught off guard by that spectral tempest

(everybody except the Crying Boy—
Doc says it's because his tears refract
and distort the light so he couldn't see
it transform but I believe that
tears or no tears the Crying Boy
saw the light only he saw it different
because he knows stuff that we don't)

and everybody felt something new
and important had happened
though I still don't get why
nobody ever said much about it.

Lenny and I didn't know that
Mayor Bob had just made his first
pilgrimage to Pilgrim Hill
to beseech the high sky powers to smile
on our little town and bring us
a bountiful harvest of rainwater
and almonds and apricots and
tax money to fix our roads.

We didn't know that Bob was up there
or that his Great Sacrifice was
under way and it turns out nobody knew
except his wife Estelle. When he headed
out the door Estelle poured herself
a scotch and ginger ale and cursed Bob
and then she prayed for him.

Nobody knew Bob had been
possessed by an unearthly demon
or that his heart had ripened and
stewed like a peach on a rooftop
as he manned up and drank up
the poisonous sizzle from
that light for the rest of us.

What we all saw were colors
that we'd never seen, though
maybe they are always there

(that's what Doc told me as he
spouted some mumbo science jumbo
about the torrents of light that
flood our eyes every instant
with only a few drops that
manage to worm their way
back to our feeble brains)

or maybe some interstellar spirit
had come down to our town
through Mayor Bob's sacrifice on
that Hill of Dead Soldiers
and Homeless Dreams, maybe
that bedazzling light altered
the air we breathe and the shapes
we see and a new day had arrived
for better and worse.

Whatever it was that entered our valley
that day, moving with the swagger
of a dim-witted bully, I feel certain
that it changed our town
changed who we all are and I believe
that most everybody in town
felt it though nobody talks about it
not even Doc or me anymore.

I do know that Lenny and I both saw
that shattering blaze and we both saw
the animate bones of that rhinobeast and
I believe that that was one reason
why Lenny later up and left town.
And I know that for me, well, it's why
I've stuck around all these years.

HENRY'S HORSES

The old barrel warehouse across the street
had a ceiling so high there was weather inside.
Henry Gutierrez lived there—they said
he'd been there since before the war,
though they never said which war.
He worked at Anger's garage all day
rebuilding engines, then came home
and slept a few hours, and when
he woke up after dark he'd knock back
a bowl of cereal and a couple beers.

If you looked over there at midnight you'd see
brilliant flashes coming from inside,
silent explosions, like lightning
trapped in a thunderless cage.
But it was only Henry's arc welder,
he worked all night fusing together
sheets and scraps of steel until
they seemed to breathe and shake
and prance and strike a noble pose.
He built animals, mostly horses,
and he said he knew he'd finished one
when he found himself talking to it.

One time Uncle Jack, my father's brother,
invited Henry to his church, the one
where they forgive you for anything
as long as you let Jesus into your heart
and drop a twenty in the basket.
But Henry knew there was no forgiving
his sins, and it made him sick
to talk about the people he'd injured
then listen to the other craven souls

56

tell him he was absolved. He said
he had his own way of atoning that
was mostly about wrestling with steel.

For some reason Henry liked being around
my father, and he was one of the few
who could make Dad smile.
Henry saw something in him,
something decent and funny and odd.
He was the first to call Dad the Pale Man,
and he was the only one
to call him that with affection.
He said he saw through the Pale Man,
literally saw through his colorless skin:
there were the slender birdbones of his legs
and there were his spidery arteries
that never glowed a full rich red
and there was the lonely lung that kept up
its wheezy bellowing after the other one
had withered with consumption. And there
was his heart with its forty-two scars.

The Pale Man acted tough and carefree
with Henry Gutierrez but they both knew
that he was neither. Henry liked him
because he talked about science,
and because he was gentle and
told the truth about everything
except his own sadness.

MENACING MUSIC

Fred Lambert, the lumber king,
and Rocky Mink, the land baron,
hated each other since junior high,
but they joined up to clear and improve
the last great stretch of savanna
this side of Rainbow Ridge. They
took out a loan from McElroy
and bought the land off those
Magnani kids whose mom and dad
had always refused to sell.

They've begun the clearing, and Sheriff Roy
put a bounty on hyenas.
Now the hunting club is out there
stalking and bagging those ugly beasts
at a century a pop.

Dorsell Quivers wants to stop them.
He wants to fence off what's left
of the savanna and keep it for
our grandkids. He says he gets such joy,
such energy running through the woods
and grasses and up Rainbow Ridge that
he can feel his spirit grow like
a beanstalk in a pig pasture.
'Let's organize a protest march
out to the townside savanna—
we'll be a platoon of Christian soldiers
fighting for all that's free and wild.'

Now there are stories of hyena maulings
and children stolen in the night,
of spiders big as fists crawling out

of the savanna grass and into
the cars and cribs of Santa Lucia.
Some even say the great reptiles from
beyond the mountain—animals only a few
humans claim to have ever seen—
are approaching the townside savanna
and scaring the hyenas our way.

Mink and Lambert talk about
the savanna like it's history.
They say it's part of our heritage
and should be remembered with
little parks and videos. They
will build a Savanna Museum, and
they've hired Phyllis Schenk to craft
a bronze hyena to stand and snarl
silently in the parking lot.

My former best friend Lenny Schacter
has money and land and I asked him
if he could help save the savanna.
He told me he already has cash
tied up in the Mink and Lambert mall
that's going up in the meadow behind
Anger's junkyard, where the hyenas
still grunt and cluck and whinny and moan.
But he'll think about it, he says,
and I believe him—Lenny loves
the savanna, and we both grew up
with the menacing music of hyenas.

THE PALE MAN

Last time I saw my dad was at
the cemetery on Pilgrim Hill,
pale as a ghost but he wasn't dead.
He stood over the grave of his grandfather,
the hero of our family.
I called out to him and waved and
he turned my way—he looked sad
and then he looked ashamed and
I felt bad for him until I understood
that his shame was directed at me.

No point in pondering his disappointment,
I know I'm a failure in his eyes and
there's no way back to the sunshine of his pride—
the boy of great promise is long dead and here I am.
And there he was—he turned away from me
and peered right through the gravestone
and into a glorious dream of the past
where a brave man stood against the mob
and brought reason to our torn-up town.

I tried to smile because I love him so much
and because I know he'll be the next to go—
that's why he was there on Pilgrim Hill
and in fact as I stood there watching
he got even paler and I could see
the silhouette of a fence post behind him,
dim x-ray of a thick dead spine.

A full moon rose in the afternoon sky.
Oh Daddy, said the scream inside my head,
oh Papa, please don't go without giving me
your blessing, the sweet sneeze of your blessing.

And then I knew that he didn't have it in him
and never had, that he was too faint and frail
and too scared to issue blessing or curse.
And I forgave him, I did my best to forgive him
and when I wake up on these fullmoon nights
that's what I do, I forgive him as best I can
because now I can't see him anymore
that's how pale he's gotten but I know
he's alive and still walks this town.

MY SISTER'S GHOST

I stepped out of Smiley's Bar and saw
my sister at the foot of Pilgrim Hill—
she was standing in front of our mother's grave.
By the time I got there she was gone.

She called to tell me
that I need to visit Aunt Rachel
in the Home for Old Jewish Ladies.
But just remember, she said,
even if you go there with flowers and chocolate
it won't be enough, because let's face it,
you don't really care.

I went to the Victoria to see
those Filipino guys dress up like ladies
and dance rumba and merengue onstage.
My sister sat down dead in front of me.
I slouched low but she turned and
spotted me, told me I was forever
shamed for stealing her happiness.
For the rest of the show all I could see
was the bald spot on the back of her head.

One time when she was in bed
with pneumonia I ambushed her,
asked her what I had done
that was so bad. At first she said
It's just who you are, you were born
deformed and dangerous and I have to
keep you on a short leash.

But she was weak with fever,
the goon squad of her personality was asleep

or off drinking and gambling in some brothel,
and after a while I wore her down.
Okay, she finally said,
you tell me what's fair:
I was always swifter than you
in mind and foot, I ran like the wind
and talked circles around you.
I had the talent to make music,
I had the gift of deep friendships.
You were a dull dumb bovine shallow clod
and then some, she said,
you asked for little and gave nothing.
Yet you have a house, a family,
a life that stinks of satisfaction.

As much as I hate her and the stunts
she pulls to smother my spirit
I didn't have the heart to tell her
that she must have mistaken me
for Cousin Myron who is
healthy, wealthy, and wise.
I am none of that, never was,
I am last week's crabmeat
I am a failing bank
a postman with an empty sack
the faint ember of a fiery lineage.
Sure, I had a house and a step-family
but the Sadist in the Sky
foreclosed on both of them.

Her ghost showed up in the night
to prepare me for when she dies.
Don't think you'll be off the hook then,
it said, that's only the beginning,
I'll hound you for ten thousand days
I'll badger you like a fury.

My sister shinnies the bole of an oak
confident as a bear.
I'm below her looking up
and I don't like what I see—
her tiny skirt hides nothing,
not the puckered valve of her bowel
not the livery folds of her libido
not even the mole on her buttcheek.

I'm afraid to climb anything,
but when she gets to a high branch
she calls to me to follow her up there.
Check out this view, she says,
you can see past Pilgrim Hill
to the Savanna Valley and beyond,
past the hyenas and baboons,
past all mammals, all the way out
to the terrible lizards of yore.

You know I'm no climber, I say,
I'll never get as high or see as far
as you. That's right, she says,
because you're a coward, but
just in case, I'll always be close by
watching, ready to hold you back,
even after I'm cremated
and scattered across the mall.

A month from now I'll run into her
at the Victoria and she'll deny she confided
her wicked agenda to me. She'll tell me
she just wants me to be happy,
in spite of the fact that she can never
be happy what with the burden
of her genius forever riding
on her shoulders, biting her neck and
clawing at her skull like a raccoon.

A year from now we'll celebrate
the killing of some bearded terrorist
we'll be drinking Tennessee whiskey
and doing the limbo under McElroy's Hummer
and laughing and hugging and we won't
remember much of this, we'll think
everything's okay and she'll say as much
she'll say You and I are a team
like George and Gracie
like Leopold and Loeb
a bond of titanium between us always
and always I'll watch over you my love,
my sweet younger brother,
forever and ever, I promise.

SANTA LUCIA BY STARLIGHT

Alone on the Walk of Cobbled Coins
on a crisp newmoon night I saw
starlight coming from under my feet.
The glimmer from the coins was like
no other light on earth, it looked old
and tired, as if from a long and bitter
journey, and it seemed happy to see me.

There was snow on the hills above our town
and sometimes the yap of a single coyote
trickled down, and I was on my way home
from a girl who no longer cared for me.
She said it wasn't my low station in life,
nor my quiet ways, but rather the slump
of my shoulders and the defeat
in my eyes that closed her heart.

My foot knocked loose a coin and I
knelt down: it was an old half-dollar
with Lady Liberty in her silver gown.
She was walking too, away from me
and with a purpose, and she glowed
like a candle at the back of a cave.
I'd heard about the curse that falls
on anyone who takes a cobbled coin,
but I wanted to hold on to the ancient light
that shone from Liberty's dress,
I needed it to help me find my way
through the dark times ahead.

I know every living room and kitchen
in every house on that street, can even
stir up their smells in my mind's nose,

66

and I was thinking maybe it's time to leave,
to climb into my old Comanche pickup
and head north to the Trinity Alps
or further north to the Cascades
or even up to Alaska where
a man can make a good living.

Holding Liberty in my hand,
I ran my finger along her fat arm,
over her breast and down her leg
to her foot, forever frozen in
its sandal and forever walking
toward a dagger-beamed sun,
and I wondered if I will ever
up and leave this town.

I put the coin and its curse back
in place with the other shimmering
change, then stood and shut my eyes.
The Walk of Coins runs east-to-west,
underneath that messy stripe
we call the Milky Way, and
every now and then there is
that special light you can walk on,
that lets you see close and deep
and dares you to step without fear.

THE BOY ON THE RIDGE

I rode my bike down from Pilgrim Hill
toward the river that splits our town.
Along the way I waved to Sheriff Roy
and Mildred Floss, then wondered what
they were saying about me and my family.

It was fall and the road was littered
with goose shit and hyena shit and
shit-shadows shrinking in the rising sun,
and Estelle was bringing milk and muffins
to Mayor Bob's bedside and pretending
his soul was alive inside its doltish husk
and my Noni was sitting in the bathtub
like a pile of wet clothes while Grappa
lay in bed dreaming of blood-hungry Cossacks
cruising the Steppe on thundering horses
and the town was still quiet enough
that you could hear the river's bashful giggle.
I was headed to my shop
to build a desk for McElroy.

Up on Pilgrim Hill my mother's voice
had spoken to me from her grave
in the Jewish section, had told me
about a little boy of few delights
and many sorrows who roams the high ridge
where Dorsell Quivers chases fox and deer.
My mother's voice said only she
can see that little boy right now,
but he'll saunter down and climb into
the belly of a comely maiden
as soon as I'm ready to be his dad.

I don't want a boy of many sorrows,
I was such a boy and my heart
isn't big enough to bear another,
to blaze the cul-de-sac of his youth
or watch his terror of his own hungry body
and the other demons of his undoing
hound him from his destiny.

But the voice of my mother who is
in death still taller and wiser than me
told me that my demons aren't
the only ones that haunt this valley
and that my feral future boy has
a destiny beyond my knowing
not to mention my days on this earth.

And yes my mom is always right
and this was no exception but
I think I'll wait a while before
I climb the Hill to visit her again
even though her nagging voice is
my one solace in this painful time.

I pushed forward on my bike
rode the bumpy rhythms of Skelter Lane
down to the south side where I was born
and where I will remain. I have to make
that desk for McElroy and a fancy
toilet seat for Lenny Schacter, and
my own destiny lies here on the south side
like a coiled python poised
to squeeze and swallow and digest.

I'll keep dancing with that snake
as long as I can, and I will make
a toilet seat like no other, cocobolo
mortised tight then jigsawed oval

and inlaid with hyenas of birdseye maple
chasing zebrawood zebras,
and on the lid the ashen face of
that boy who is a dead ringer
for my dad, the Pale Man.

ALIEN BELLS

When you die you won't know you're dead.
You'll just lie there, drunk as the worm in your nostril,
humming every song you ever heard,
until a warm wind bathes your skin
and a single thought stretches thin as a spider's dream
as every door in your body opens
to the swarm that loves you.
Then your memories will shake loose and fall
and keep on falling until they are everywhere
and *you* will be falling, although you won't know it,
you'll be growing and falling in a dry swirl
of color and dust and the smell of burning hair.

The next time you die it will be a merciful blur,
an anesthetic yawn that carries you
to the town that broke my heart,
the town that breaks my heart every day—
you'll be standing there on the street and then
you'll start walking, slowly, like a pilgrim,
one resurrected foot in front of the other.

I'll bump into you then. I'll know you
like an old song and invite you into my home
and feed you soup and sliced bread
and give you the cap and scarf my sister knitted
and watch you closely, waiting for something.

I'll keep watching, and maybe I'll get closer
and smell the damp wool of your shirt,
see the hairs growing on your moles,
hear your lungs whistle as you breathe.
I'll tell you the beginnings of stories,
hoping you'll take over and spit some life

into them so they can get up and walk
by themselves and find their way toward
that slippery staircase called The End.

I'll beg you to bless my family with an old prayer,
spoken in Hebrew or some forgotten tongue,
and I'll sniff your breath as you speak
and then I'll know what Hebrew smells like.

I'll have only one question to ask you, and that is
Did all those wasted years shrink my soul?
And I'll have only one more question, and that is
Can I love my child even as he laughs in my face?
And one more: Is it really my fault?

But by then you'll be on your way,
finding your way out of Santa Lucia
and back to a staid shtetl on another continent
where you can be a child and wake up
to the alien bells of a distant limestone church.
And one day you'll watch the colors in the sky
congregate in an anxious shimmer, a vision,
an angel, and you'll drop to your knees
on a sharp-graveled road and pray for all of us:
me, my family, you and your many selves,
and the road, yes, the road that bloodies
your knees and strings our lives together.

ACKNOWLEDGMENTS

"My Father's Brother" and "The Crying Boy" appeared in *Dogwood*, Spring 2010. "My Father's Brother" won the *Dogwood* Poetry Prize, 2010 (selected by Marilyn Hacker).

"Henry's Horses," "The Pale Man," and "The Boy on the Ridge" appeared in *New Ohio Review* 20, Fall 2016. The group of three poems won the *NOR* Poetry Contest for 2016 (selected by Tony Hoagland).

"Great Big Woman" and "Noni and Grappa" appeared in *Juked*, Spring 2017.

"Alien Bells" appeared in *Confrontation* 122, Fall 2017.

Michael Pearce has worked as a furniture designer and builder, a university lecturer, and as Director of Cognition Exhibits at the Exploratorium, the San Francisco science museum. His poems and stories have been published widely. He lives in Oakland, California, and plays saxophone in the Bay Area band Highwater Blues.

CPSIA information can be obtained
at www.ICGtesting.com
Printed in the USA
LVHW100716280223
740531LV00010B/38